The Powhatan

A Confederacy of Native American Tribes

by Tracey Boraas

Consultant:
Chief Roy Crazy Horse, Executive Director
Powhatan Renape Nation
Rankokus Indian Reservation
Rancocas, New Jersey

Bridgestone Books

an imprint of Capstone Press
Mankato, Minnesota

Bridgestone Books are published by Capstone Press
151 Good Counsel Drive • P.O. Box 669 • Mankato, Minnesota 56002
http://www.capstone-press.com

Library of Congress Cataloging-in-Publication Data
Boraas, Tracey.
    The Powhatan: A confederacy of Native American tribes/by
Tracey Boraas.
        p. cm. — (American Indian nations)
    Summary: Provides an overview of the past and present lives of
the Powhatan people, tracing their customs, family life, history,
culture, and relations with English settlers.
    Includes bibliographical references and index.
    ISBN 0-7368-1567-8 (hardcover)
    1. Powhatan Indians—Juvenile literature. [1. Powhatan Indians.
2. Indians of North America—Virginia.] I. Title. II. Series.
E99.P85 B67 2003
975'.004973—dc21   2002012003

Editorial Credits
Charles Pederson, editor; Kia Adams, designer; Alta Schaffer, photo
researcher; Karen Risch, product planning editor

Photo Credits
Capstone Press/Gary Sundermeyer, 15
Corbis/Bettmann, 22, 35
Hulton Archive by Getty Images, 24–25
Jan Lucie, 36
Kit Breen, 21, 40
Marilyn "Angel" Wynn, cover (main and inset), 4, 8, 13, 17, 38, 42, 44,
45
North Wind Picture Archives, 18, 29, 31, 33
Stock Montage, Inc., 11, 26

1 2 3 4 5 6 08 07 06 05 04 03

Table of Contents

Features

A modern memorial on the Pamunkey Reservation in Virginia shows an image of Chief Powhatan. He led the powerful Powhatan Confederacy in the late 1500s.

Chapter One

Who Are the Powhatan?

The first Powhatan originally were a small, powerful nation of American Indians. They lived on the coast of what later became Virginia. Chief Wahunsonacock, later called Powhatan, led the Powhatan nation. He united more than 30 tribes in the region to form the Powhatan Confederacy. These tribes included the Pamunkey, Rappahannock, Nansemond, and Mattaponi.

The tribes of the Powhatan Confederacy shared similar traditions and cultures. They spoke forms of the Algonquian language. They lived in forest villages. The climate was one of cold winters and warm summers. The Powhatan hunted and farmed, growing beans, squash, a kind of corn called maize, and other vegetables.

In 1607, people from England settled a village called Jamestown. The settlement was in Powhatan territory. The Powhatan were friendly and helpful to the first Jamestown colonists. The Powhatan shared maize with the starving English settlers. But more colonists kept arriving in Powhatan territory. They fought the Powhatan for the land. The Powhatan caught deadly diseases from the colonists.

At the time of English settlement, the Powhatan Confederacy included up to 14,000 people. It covered much of present-day Virginia. After many years, the confederacy became weak from fighting with the colonists. Tribes broke away, and the Powhatan Confederacy ended. Individual tribes struggled for many years against the English.

During the mid-1900s, several hundred Indians who descended from the original Powhatan united. They formed a new Powhatan Confederacy on the Rankokus Indian Reservation in New Jersey. Other former confederacy tribes live in nearby Virginia. All of these people have a renewed pride in their history.

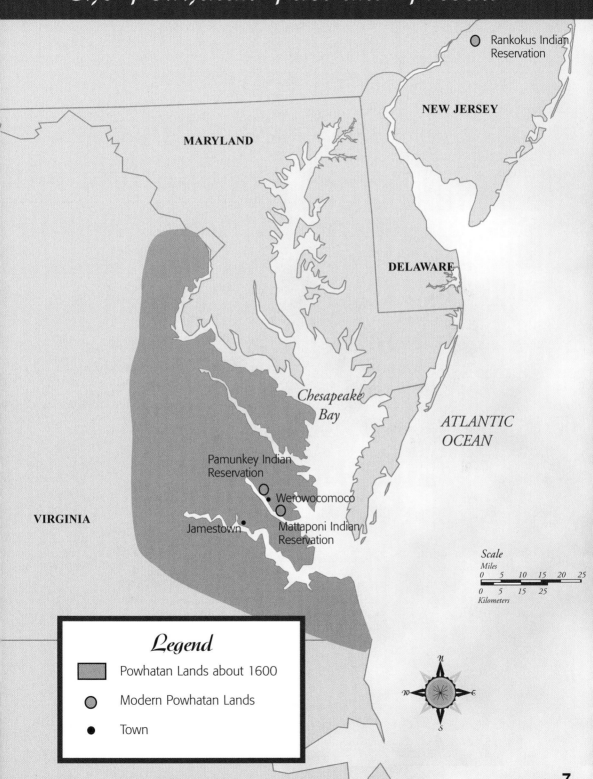

Rankokus Indian
Reservation

NEW JERSEY

MARYLAND

DELAWARE

Chesapeake
Bay

ATLANTIC
OCEAN

Pamunkey Indian
Reservation

Werowocomoco

VIRGINIA

Jamestown

Mattaponi Indian
Reservation

Scale
Miles
0   5   10   15   20   25
0   5   15   25
Kilometers

Legend

Powhatan Lands about 1600

Modern Powhatan Lands

Town

N
W   E
S

7

A tall fence called a palisade sometimes surrounded Powhatan villages.

Chapter Two

Traditional Life

The Powhatan had lived on their lands
along the central Atlantic Coast thousands
of years before settlers arrived. More than
30 Indian groups were part of the Powhatan
Confederacy. These people lived in what
became Virginia and Maryland, near the
Chesapeake Bay.

Powhatan who lived in forests built
small villages of 20 or fewer longhouses.
Some of these villages were surrounded by
a high fence called a palisade. The palisade
was made of wooden poles. Most houses in
a village had one large room with a door at
each end. A fire was kept burning in the
house at all times. A hole in the roof
allowed smoke from the fire to escape. The

walls had mats that could be rolled up to let sunlight and fresh air enter the houses.

Only a little is known about Powhatan government. Chiefs called werowances (WIHR-uh-wanz-uhz) were in charge of villages. A tribal werowance led several villages. Villagers paid taxes to their werowance. Village werowances paid taxes to their tribal werowance. An important leader called a mamanatowick (mam-an-uh-TOH-wik) ruled over many tribes in the confederacy. The tribal werowances paid taxes to him.

Spiritual leaders helped the werowances make important decisions. These leaders also acted as doctors. They made medicines from plants, roots, and other items from nature to help sick people.

Village leaders who were not werowances met together as a group called a council. The council helped the werowances make decisions for the entire Powhatan Confederacy.

Family Life

The Powhatan lived along the coast in an area of lowlands known as the Tidewater. Rivers that flow into the Chesapeake Bay cover this area. The ocean tides bring salty ocean water up these rivers and mix it with the fresh river water.

The Powhatan built their villages on high ground along these rivers. Their homes were scattered about the village among small fields. If the nearby river was salty, the Powhatan used a spring to get fresh drinking water.

Families of children, parents, and grandparents often shared a home. Many people in a village were related to one another. Families shared in the work and helped take care of each other.

Women's Roles

Women did many jobs in a village. They made clay pots and tools, wove mats and baskets, and wove plant fibers into

Powhatan villages were full of busy people. They cooked by fires, tended their fields, and did other jobs to help the people in the village.

rope. They cleaned and prepared animal hides to make leather for clothing. Women did most of the village's cooking.

Women were in charge of building longhouses. Powhatan longhouses were made of two rows of young, springy trees called saplings. The saplings were stuck into the ground and then bent and tied together at the top to form a tunnel-shaped frame. The women tied larger poles sideways across the saplings. They then covered this frame with mats of grass and tree bark. Sheets of bark sealed with grass were used as a roof.

Men's Roles

Powhatan men were skilled hunters. They supplied meat for food and skins for clothing. The Powhatan hunted muskrats, rabbits, squirrels, raccoons, wild turkeys, bears, and deer. They used wooden bows with a tight string made of twisted animal gut. Their arrows had sharp tips made of stone, bone, bird beaks, or even deer antlers.

The Powhatan were clever deer hunters. Deer provided most Powhatan food. The men sometimes disguised themselves by covering their backs with deerskin. The disguise helped the hunter get close enough to deer to shoot an arrow at them. Hunters sometimes formed a large circle around a herd of deer. They built fires between each man, then shouted and frightened the deer. The deer tried to escape but could not because the men and fires surrounded them. The deer ran until exhausted. The hunters then could shoot as many as they needed. Hunters sometimes forced deer into water. Other men in canoes shot these deer.

Powhatan men chose their own marriage partners. A man gave a woman meat from a game animal he had killed. The gift was the way he asked her to marry him. It also proved he

A modern Powhatan man shows the hunting method of draping a deerskin over himself.

would be a good provider. If the woman accepted his gift, the man met with her parents to decide when to get married.

Children's Roles

Adults trained children from a young age for traditional Powhatan duties. Women helped teach boys to be skilled hunters. Mothers threw a target into the air each morning for their sons to shoot with arrows. A mother might not allow her son to eat breakfast until he hit the target. Girls learned to cook, farm, and do other things their mothers did. Children watched adults to learn how to behave.

Powhatan children learned through stories, songs, and play. From storytellers, the children learned the history of their people. Music was important to the Powhatan. Children learned to make music with deerskin drums, cane flutes, and dried-gourd rattles. Children, as well as adults, played stickball, danced, wrestled, ran footraces, and played other games.

Food

During summer and fall, the Powhatan gathered food. They prepared and stored it for use during the rest of the year. They stored some food beside the house on a rack called a

Clam Chowder

The Powhatan depended on the rivers, lakes, and ocean around them for many kinds of food. They ate fish and other seafood, including a clam soup called a chowder. Ask an adult to help you cook the recipe below.

Ingredients

2 teaspoons (10 mL) vegetable oil
¾ cup (175 mL) onions, chopped
1–2 stalks celery, chopped
1 tablespoon (15 mL) flour
2 large potatoes, peeled and diced
¼ teaspoon (1.2 mL) thyme
1 6-ounce (180-gram) can of clams,
   saving liquid

¾ cup (175 mL) clam juice or water
1 tablespoon (15 mL) butter
¼ teaspoon (1.2 mL) salt and pepper
1½ cups (360 mL) milk
½ cup (120 mL) half-and-half or milk
¼ pound (110 grams) bacon, cooked
   and chopped
½ teaspoon (2.5 mL) parsley

Equipment

kitchen knife
large saucepan
wooden stirring spoon
liquid-ingredient measuring cup

measuring cups
measuring spoons
5 serving bowls

What You Do

1. Pour oil into saucepan and heat over medium high heat.
2. Add chopped onions and celery. Cook about 2 minutes, or until onions are soft.
3. Quickly sprinkle flour over onions and celery. Stir to coat vegetables.
4. Add potatoes, thyme, liquid from can of clams, clam juice, butter, salt, and pepper. Reduce heat to medium and cook uncovered until potatoes are tender, about 10–15 minutes. Stir occasionally during cooking.
5. Add milk, half-and-half, clams, and bacon. Stir over medium heat until hot.
6. Pour soup into bowls, add parsley on top of soup, and serve.

Serves about 5

scaffold. They stored other food in specially prepared and lined holes in the ground.

As the weather grew cooler, people got ready for the long winter hunt. Everyone except the young and old headed west for this hunt. For several months, men hunted, and women tended temporary homes. The women also cooked meals and worked animal skins into leather for clothing. When spring returned, the Powhatan went back to their home village to begin the season of planting.

Farming was the main job in any village. Women, children, and some older men worked the fields each spring. They planted tobacco to use in spiritual and political ceremonies. They planted a type of corn called maize. They also grew beans, squash, and other vegetables.

Maize was an important crop to the Powhatan. They grew different types of maize that ripened from early June to October. Maize was eaten roasted, ground, and boiled. The cornstalks contained sweet juice that the Powhatan sucked. Women dried maize for the winter by laying it on mats in the sun. The Powhatan always saved some maize seeds for planting season the next spring.

Powhatan Canoes

Canoes were an important part of Powhatan life. The Powhatan used canoes for fishing, hunting, and traveling the rivers of the Tidewater area.

The Powhatan made their canoes by hollowing out logs. They hollowed logs by burning small sections of them. They then scraped out the burned material with stone axes. They repeated the burning and scraping until the canoe was finished. Canoes could be as long as 50 feet (15 meters) and could hold up to 40 people. The canoe below is a modern reconstruction of a traditional Powhatan canoe.

Nature provided food throughout the year. In spring, women gathered wild strawberries, raspberries, apples, and grapes in the forests. They dug wild potatoes. In the fall, they collected walnuts, hickory nuts, acorns, and chestnuts. Some nuts were used for food. Others were used for oils in cooking and in medicines.

Fishing from land or canoe, men caught fish as a regular source of meat. The Powhatan used rods with bone

Foods made from fish were an important part of the Powhatan diet. The Powhatan prepared fish by smoking them on a frame.

Powhatan Spirituality

The Powhatan were very spiritual people. Part of their spirituality was the belief that all life was holy. They respected each other and nature. They gave thanks for family, health, and the good things they had. They thanked nature for the food it provided.

Storytelling was another part of Powhatan spirituality. Children learned many things through stories. One story parents told their children was about how people came to live on Earth.

A rabbit called Hare created humans and kept them in a bag in his house. Winds came and wanted to eat the men and women, but Hare sent the winds away.

Next, Hare created water, land, and a single deer. The winds returned. They were angry and ate the deer. Hare took hairs from the dead deer and spread them across the Earth. He spoke special words and turned each hair into a deer. He then opened his bag and placed men and women in every part of the world. This was the beginning of people on Earth.

fishhooks and nets woven from rope. They sometimes shot fish with arrows tied to cords. Men also could spear fish in shallow water.

The Powhatan prepared fish in many ways. Dishes of roasted, boiled, or stewed fish were common. The Powhatan also smoked or dried fish on a frame so it could last several months without spoiling.

Clothing

As in modern society, the men, women, and children in Powhatan society had their own ways of decorating themselves. Men wore several hairstyles, including ponytails. They sometimes wore earrings made of beads, birds' feet, or animal claws. Women tattooed their faces and bodies. To tattoo themselves, they cut shallow designs into their skin with heated knives. They then rubbed ashes from a fire into the cuts to darken the lines.

The Powhatan dressed according to the weather. In the warm summers, they dressed in light clothes. In the winter, the Powhatan wore leather and fur jackets, shirts, and pants.

Leather clothing provided protection against cold temperatures. The modern Mattaponi people pictured above display traditional Powhatan clothes.

Chief Powhatan, shown standing, was a Potomac leader who united many Indian nations in the Powhatan Confederacy.

Chapter Three

Colonization and Change

In the 1520s, Spanish and Portuguese explorers first visited the Chesapeake Bay but did not stay. Around 1560, the Spanish returned and built a religious mission near the bay. They kidnapped a young American Indian man and tried to force him to live like the Spanish. The Powhatan in the area became angry and drove the Spanish from the land. Later, the English tried to colonize the area, but the Powhatan stopped them.

In the late 1500s, Chief Wahunsonacock of the Potomac Indians was the Powhatan mamanatowick. Europeans called him Chief Powhatan. He brought more than 30 tribes under his rule. This group became known as the Powhatan Confederacy.

In the spring of 1607, three English ships carrying about 100 Englishmen sailed into the Chesapeake Bay. The ships stopped at Powhatan villages along the James River. The Powhatan who greeted the English were kind and generous. They gave feasts to honor the strangers.

English settlers in Virginia, shown at center, traded with the Powhatan. The settlers built Jamestown.

The Powhatan Help

The settlers built a fort along the James River and named it Jamestown. Both the fort and river were named after the English King James I. Jamestown was located in a swampy area along the river. This location was poor. The salty river water was undrinkable. Mosquitoes swarmed the area in the summer heat.

The colonists had trouble surviving in Jamestown. By summer, these new settlers were sick from drinking bad water and from diseases carried by mosquitoes. The Jamestown colonists did not know how to hunt game. In England, hunting was illegal because all forest animals belonged to the royal family. The Powhatan taught the settlers to fish and hunt.

The colonists also did not know how to plant crops and soon ran out of food. Chief Powhatan's people taught the colonists to plant maize, beans, and squash. In return, the English gave the Powhatan needles, bells, and other trade goods.

The colonists expected a supply ship from England, but it never arrived. By the end of the summer, nearly 50 colonists had died. In 1607,

Powhatan crops were poor. But still, the Powhatan gave whatever crops they could spare to the starving colonists.

Jamestown leader Captain John Smith went on trading trips to find maize. The Powhatan became less friendly as Smith demanded more food than they could spare. In December, Chief Powhatan's brother Opechancanough (op-uh-KAN-cuh-naw) captured Smith. He took Smith to Chief Powhatan in the Powhatan capital of Werowocomoco.

When Smith wrote of his time with the Powhatan, he said that Chief Powhatan welcomed him. The chief simply asked

John Smith, a Jamestown leader, traded with the Powhatan for food the colonists needed.

Smith why the English had come and how long they would stay. Smith told the chief the English ships were damaged. He added that the colonists would stay only until the ships were repaired. Smith lied. Actually, the colonists never planned to leave.

Time passed, but the settlers showed no signs of leaving. They continued to need food from the Powhatan, but harvests continued to be poor. The Powhatan people barely had enough for themselves.

Finally, the colonists started raiding Indian villages for food. They took part of the winter supplies from the Powhatan. As a result, Powhatan warriors attacked Jamestown.

Supplies and New Settlers

The colonists finally decided to leave Jamestown. In May 1610, they boarded their ships and set sail for England. After one day at sea, the colonists spotted an English ship headed toward Jamestown. It was part of a fleet that carried supplies and 300 new settlers. With supplies and many new settlers, the first colonists returned to Jamestown.

The colonists started new settlements near Jamestown. They no longer tried to get along with the Powhatan. They burned Powhatan fields and killed entire villages of people. The Powhatan fought back by attacking English settlements.

The Failing Empire

The strength of the Powhatan Confederacy rapidly faded during the last years of Chief Powhatan's rule. These years were marked by poor harvests, hunger, and disease. Powhatan were unfamiliar with smallpox, measles, tuberculosis, and other European diseases. These deadly diseases spread across the land and killed many Powhatan.

In 1618, Chief Powhatan died. His brother Opichapam became mamanatowick. He was not a strong chief. Chief Powhatan's other brother, Opechancanough, soon took over from Opichapam as mamanatowick.

The English population continued to grow as more settlers came to North America. By 1622, the English population rose to 1,240 people. The English continued to take Powhatan land.

The English wanted the Powhatan to become Christians. They forced Powhatan children to live with English families and learn Christian religious practices.

Chief Opechancanough made a plan to drive the English from Powhatan lands. The settlers allowed unarmed Powhatan men to enter English settlements to trade and work. On March 22, 1622, the chief sent Powhatan to the settlements. The Powhatan grabbed the colonists' weapons and attacked the colonists. By the end of the day, they had killed 330 colonists.

Opechancanough thought the English would be so scared, they would leave. Instead, the English fought back. They

Chief Opechancanough gestured while describing a plan to drive
the English settlers from Powhatan land.

burned Powhatan crops and villages and smashed canoes. They killed any Indians they met.

In May 1623, Opechancanough and other Powhatan met with the English to discuss peace. The English gave the Powhatan a drink they had secretly poisoned. The Powhatan became ill, and many died. Opechancanough was poisoned but did not die. He was able to return to his people.

War Years

Times of war and peace continued for about 20 years. During those years, the English population grew to more than 8,000 people. Disease and hunger reduced the Powhatan population to fewer than 5,000.

In 1644, Opechancanough made a final attempt to push the colonists from Powhatan land. His warriors attacked settlements and killed 400 settlers. The English led their own attacks against the Powhatan. After the attacks, the Powhatan no longer had enough men to fight.

In 1646, the English captured the 80-year-old Chief Opechancanough. When he refused to sign a peace treaty, the English shot and killed him.

That same year, the next mamanatowick, Nectowance, signed a treaty with the English. The treaty put the Powhatan under the rule of the English king. The treaty demanded a yearly tax of 20 beaver skins paid to the colonial governor.

The treaty also gave the English all Powhatan land between the James and York Rivers. Nectowance's messengers could enter the area if they wore striped shirts to signal who they were. The English shot other Indians entering the area. By 1649, the Powhatan Confederacy no longer existed.

More Land for the English

Many English farmers grew tobacco, which used up the nutrients in the farmland. The English wanted more land from the Powhatan.

English colonists in Virginia fought for many years with the Powhatan.

Finally, some tribal werowances asked the colonial government to protect land for their people. The government set aside reservations that were only for Powhatan to use.

Some settlers ignored reservation boundaries. They moved onto the lands to grow tobacco. The colonial government did not stop these settlers. The Indians were forced into smaller areas of land. The reservations became so small that the Powhatan could no longer support themselves by hunting. They barely had enough land to farm. Some Powhatan moved away from the area.

Other Powhatan worked for the colonists as servants. Powhatan parents with no way to feed their families sent their children to work for English families. The English often treated these children like slaves.

The Powhatan did whatever they could to earn money. Women sold baskets and pottery. Men worked as hunters for settlers to kill wolves that might harm farm animals.

In the 1670s, tobacco prices dropped. The English settlers felt poor and open to Indian attacks. They attacked and captured a group of Powhatan. These Powhatan escaped from the fort where they were prisoners. They organized a group to attack English settlements.

The colonists then attacked the Powhatan tribes. One group of settlers forced a Pamunkey tribe from its village. The

During the 1670s, the English took Powhatan people prisoner.

English killed many Pamunkey villagers in a nearby swamp. Other Pamunkey were captured and taken to Jamestown as prisoners.

In 1677, the English and Powhatan signed a new treaty. The Powhatan repeated their agreement to live under the English king's rule. New, even smaller reservations were set aside for the Powhatan. Still, some colonists ignored the boundaries and moved onto these reservations.

A Disappearing Culture

Fewer than 1,000 Powhatan people survived into the early 1700s. These survivors were losing their culture. Moccasin, raccoon, and some other words were among the few Powhatan words still used. Most of the people learned to speak English. They wore English-style clothing made from cloth. They hunted with guns as the English did. Many Powhatan became Christians.

Powhatan tribes continued to lose reservation land to settlers. Some tribes joined together to form new groups. Other tribes split apart, and their members moved to other areas. By the early 1800s, only the Pamunkey and Accomac tribes still had reservations. They were the only Powhatan tribes the Virginia government legally recognized.

Pocahontas (Matoaka)

Pocahontas was born in 1595. She was a daughter of Chief Powhatan. Her true name was Matoaka, but many of her people called her Pocahontas. In the Powhatan language, "Pocahontas" means playful one.

In 1607, English people built Jamestown in Powhatan territory. Pocahontas convinced her people to give food to the starving colonists. Although the Powhatan shared their food, they did not always have a good relationship with the colonists.

In 1612, the English kidnapped Pocahontas. They wanted land from the Powhatan in exchange for Pocahontas' return. Chief Powhatan refused to trade. The colonists held Pocahontas prisoner for one year.

As a prisoner, Pocahontas learned about English culture and became a Christian. She received the name Rebecca. Her 1614 marriage to John Rolfe brought a few years of peace between the Powhatan and the colonists. Pocahontas and Rolfe had a son, Thomas.

In 1616, Pocahontas and her family sailed to England and stayed for one year. She met the king, queen, and other important English people. In the picture to the right, painted about 1616, she wore English clothes. In 1617, Pocahontas planned to return to Virginia but died of tuberculosis before leaving England. She was buried in southeast England.

The powwow dancer in yellow belongs to the Chickahominy people. The Chickahominy are descendants of a Powhatan Confederacy tribe.

Chapter Four

The Powhatan Today

After the U.S. Civil War (1861–1865), the Pamunkey were the only Powhatan tribe Virginia officially recognized as American Indians. The Pamunkey worked hard to keep this status. They demanded better schools. They started their own churches.

Other Powhatan tribes worked to receive recognition from Virginia as Indian tribes. In the 1920s, Virginia officially recognized the Mattaponi as a tribe. The government gave them their own reservation.

Virginia's strict laws made life difficult for many Powhatan. Some Powhatan moved to northeastern states where they hoped for better treatment. One of these groups was the Powhatan Renape Nation. These descendants of the Powhatan Confederacy live on the Rankokus Indian Reservation in New Jersey.

Today, descendants of the Powhatan Confederacy live all across the United States. Many still live close to their Virginia homeland.

Virginia today recognizes several tribes that were part of the Powhatan Confederacy. These tribes include the

The Mattaponi River runs through the Pamunkey Reservation in Virginia. The Pamunkey Reservation was created in the 1600s.

Curtis L. "War Horse" Custalow Sr.

Chief Curtis L. "War Horse" Custalow Sr. was born on June 26, 1916. Custalow was a member of the Mattaponi people, who belonged to the original Powhatan Confederacy. Custalow was educated on the Mattaponi Reservation in Virginia.

Custalow served as a U.S. soldier in Europe during World War II (1939–1945). He was wounded during the Battle of the Bulge. During his military service, he received three Bronze Stars, a Marksmanship Medal, and the Good Conduct Medal.

After the war, Custalow operated his own trucking and logging business. In 1969, he was elected chief of the Mattaponi. As chief, he promoted the good of his nation and all American Indians. He served as chief until 1977.

Custalow served on the board of an organization that represents Indians, the Native American Rights Fund. He also served the Powhatan Confederacy and several other groups that help Indians. He remained an active member of the Mattaponi Council until his death on September 6, 2001.

Pamunkey, Upper Mattaponi, Rappahannock, Mattaponi, Chickahominy, and Nansemond. The Pamunkey and Mattaponi reservations are the oldest in the United States. Each tribe has its own government to serve its people in a modern society.

As in the past, families today are very important to the modern Powhatan. Parents want their children to know what being Powhatan means.

Chapter Five

Sharing the Traditions

Over the past 400 years, the Powhatan have overcome many hardships. They have struggled against a culture that tried to wipe out their existence. Although the Powhatan survived, they almost lost their American Indian culture.

Modern Powhatan live like many other North Americans. They own homes, attend school, and go to work. Some Powhatan work in government positions. Others have become doctors, lawyers, and teachers.

Today's descendants of the original Powhatan work hard to continue their culture. Some Powhatan practice traditional spiritual beliefs. The Powhatan Renape continue to use the Powhatan language.

The Pamunkey Indians carry on the Powhatan culture through their pottery. For hundreds of years, they have made bowls, pots, and pipes of clay. Today, the Pamunkey Indian Reservation is home to a pottery school where Powhatan women continue this craft. At one time, some potters moved

Displaying pottery is one way the Pamunkey Indian Museum in King William, Virginia, shares Powhatan traditions with other people.

away from their traditional Pamunkey method of creating pots from coiled clay ropes. Instead, they used modern tools and designs. Today, many Pamunkey have returned to the traditional coiling method.

Many Powhatan tribe members work to teach non-Indian people about traditional Powhatan culture. They have built museums and art galleries on their reservations. Thousands of schoolchildren and adults visit these reservations each year to learn about the Powhatan.

The tribes hold special festivals to display their culture and history. The Upper Mattaponi hold a yearly spring festival that is open to the public. The Powhatan Renape Nation holds the American Indian Arts Festival each spring. It is the largest festival of its kind east of the Mississippi River. The Powhatan Renape also hold a festival each August. During the festival, they perform a play about the true story of Pocahontas. This is a different story from the one most people know.

The Powhatan once had to give up much of their culture. Today, they proudly practice their traditional customs, language, and crafts. They want to continue these traditions and pass them on to their children and future generations.

Powhatan Timeline

English colonists
found Jamestown.

The English kidnap
Pocahontas and take her
to live in Jamestown.

Chief Powhatan dies

| Late 1500s | 1607 | 1612 | 1617 | 1618 |

Chief Powhatan
creates the Powhatan
Confederacy and rules
more than 30 tribes.

Pocahontas dies.

A treaty is signed putting the Powhatan under the English king's rule.

Virginia recognizes the Pamunkey, Rappahannock, Mattaponi, Upper Mattaponi, Chickahominy, and Eastern Chickahominy groups of the original Powhatan Confederacy as official tribes.

1646   **1920s**   **1983**   **1985**

Virginia recognizes the Nansemond as an official tribe.

Virginia officially recognizes the Mattaponi as an American Indian tribe.

Glossary

ceremony (SER-uh-moh-nee)—traditional words or actions used to celebrate a special occasion

confederacy (kuhn-FED-ur-uh-see)—a union of towns or tribes with a common goal

mamanatowick (mam-an-uh-TOH-wik)—the most important chief of the Powhatan

migrate (MYE-grate)—to move from one region to another

tradition (truh-DISH-uhn)—a custom, idea, or belief that is handed down from one generation to the next

werowance (WIHR-uh-wanz)—a Powhatan chief

Internet Sites

Track down many sites about the Powhatan. Visit the FACT HOUND at *http://www.facthound.com*. IT IS EASY! IT IS FUN!

1) Go to *http://www.facthound.com*
2) Type in: 0736815678
3) Click on "FETCH IT," and FACT HOUND will find several links hand-picked by our editors.

Relax and let our pal FACT HOUND do the research for you!

Places to Write and Visit

Jamestown Settlement
Jamestown-Yorktown Foundation
P.O. Box 1607
Williamsburg, VA 23187

Pamunkey Indian Museum
Route 1
P.O. Box 2011
King William, VA 23086

Powhatan Renape Nation's
American Indian Heritage Museum
P.O. Box 225
Rancocas, NJ 08073

For Further Reading

Ansary, Mir Tamim. *Eastern Woodlands Indians.* Native Americans. Chicago: Heinemann Library, 2000.

Bial, Raymond. *The Powhatan.* Lifeways. New York: Marshall Cavendish/Benchmark Books, 2000.

Collier, Christopher. *The Paradox of Jamestown, 1585–1700.* The Drama of American History. New York: Benchmark Books, 1998.

Index